HEAT

Troll Associates

HEAT

by Laurence Santrey

Illustrated by Lloyd Birmingham

Troll Associates

Library of Congress Cataloging in Publication Data

Santrey, Laurence.
  Heat.

  Summary: Discusses such aspects of heat as temperature,
molecular activity, the laws of thermodynamics,
conduction, convection, radiation, and calories.
  1. Heat—Juvenile literature. [1. Heat] I. Birmingham, Lloyd, ill. II. Title.
QC256.S26   1985   536   84-2711
ISBN 0-8167-0306-X (lib. bdg.)
ISBN 0-8167-0307-8 (pbk.)

Copyright © 1985 by Troll Associates, Mahwah, New Jersey
All rights reserved. No part of this book may be used
or reproduced in any manner whatsoever without written
permission from the publisher.
Printed in the United States of America
10 9 8 7 6 5 4 3 2 1

We say a bowl of soup is hot, and we say an ice cube is cold. We say a fire is hot and a glass of lemonade is cold. But we know that the fire is a lot hotter than the bowl of soup, and an ice cube is colder than the lemonade. So what do we really mean when we say something is hot or cold?

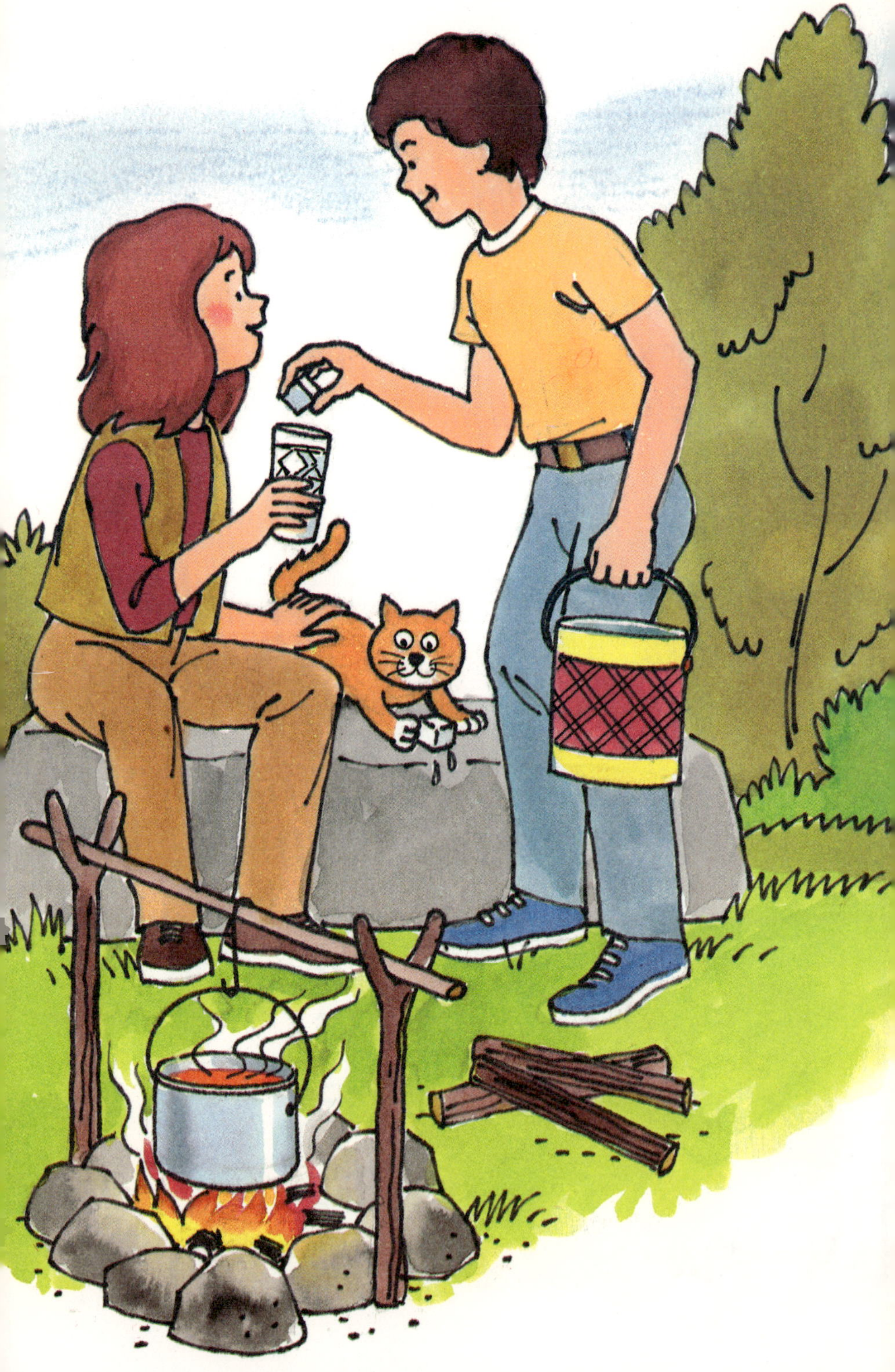

Usually, when we call something hot or cold, we are comparing its temperature to the temperature of our bodies. Temperature is the measure of heat and cold. The temperatures of the soup and the fire are higher than the temperature of our bodies. So we say the soup and the fire are hot. The temperatures of the ice cube and the lemonade are lower than the temperature of our bodies. So we say that the lemonade and ice cube are cold.

But you can't really measure the temperature of something by comparing it to your body temperature. And you can't always tell how hot or cold things are by touching them.

You can do an experiment to prove this. You need a bowl of hot water, a bowl of cold water, and a bowl of warm water. If you put one hand into the bowl of hot water, it will make that hand feel hot. If you put your other hand into the cold water, it will make *that* hand feel cold.

Then, if you put both hands into the warm water, something interesting happens. The warm water feels cold to the hand that was in the hot water. But it feels hot to the hand that was in the cold water. Yet no matter how it feels to your hands, the warm water is warm, not hot or cold.

11

Because we cannot trust our sense of touch, we have a scientific tool for measuring temperature. It is called a thermometer. There are many kinds of thermometers, but the kind we see most of the time is a glass tube with a colored liquid in it. When the temperature goes up, the liquid—which is usually the element called mercury—expands. As it expands, it fills more of the tube. When the temperature goes down, the mercury contracts, or gets smaller, and fills less of the tube.

Some thermometers are attached to a board that has lines and numbers on it. Other thermometers have the lines and numbers right on the glass tube. The lines and numbers show us degrees of temperature the way the lines and numbers on a ruler show us inches or centimeters.

There are two scales used to measure temperature. One is the Fahrenheit scale, named for its inventor, Gabriel Fahrenheit, a German scientist. On the Fahrenheit scale, water freezes at 32 degrees and boils at 212 degrees. The normal temperature of the human body on the Fahrenheit scale is between 98 and 99 degrees.

Celsius scale:
Water boils at 100°

Fahrenheit scale:
Water freezes at 32°

The other temperature scale is the Celsius scale, named for its inventor, Anders Celsius, a Swedish scientist. On the Celsius scale, also called the Centigrade scale, water freezes at zero degrees and boils at 100 degrees. On the Celsius scale, the normal temperature of the human body is about 37 degrees.

For a long time, even though people knew how to measure heat with a thermometer, they didn't know what heat was. Some early scientists said it was an invisible liquid that could flow in and out of things. Other scientists said that heat was not a thing at all. They said that it was motion.

Then an American-born scientist—Benjamin Thompson, who later became known as Count Rumford—proved that the motion theory was correct.

One day he was overseeing workers who were making a cannon. First they made a solid piece of brass. Then they bored a hole in it so that it became a long, hollow tube. As the hole was being bored, the brass became very hot. The harder the workers twisted and pushed the boring tool against the brass, the hotter it grew.

When the work stopped, the brass cooled. When the work started again, the brass got hot again. From these facts, Count Rumford decided that the work energy—or mechanical energy—of boring the cannon was changed into heat.

You can change mechanical energy into heat just by rubbing your hands together quickly. After a short time they will begin to feel warm. This is what happened to the brass.

Here is how motion, like rubbing two hands together, makes heat. Your hands are made of molecules. So is everything else in the universe. Molecules are bits of matter too small to be seen even under the strongest microscopes. When you rub your hands together, the motion makes the molecules in your hands move around quickly. This molecular activity is heat. The faster and harder you rub things together, the more the molecules move, which produces greater heat.

There are three scientific rules about heat called the laws of thermodynamics. The first law says that energy can be changed from one form to another, but energy can never be created or destroyed. The mechanical energy of rubbing two hands together is changed into heat energy, and you feel your hands grow warm. When gasoline is burned in a car engine, chemical energy changes into heat energy. The heat energy is then changed into the mechanical energy that runs the engine.

The second law of thermodynamics says that heat always flows from something hot to something cooler. A glass of hot water will lose its heat into the air around it. After a while the water will be the same temperature as the air. A glass of very cold water will take in heat from the air around it until the water is the same temperature as the air.

The third law of thermodynamics says that it is possible to come very close to a temperature called absolute zero, but that it is impossible to reach it. Absolute zero is about 460 degrees below zero Fahrenheit, or about 273 degrees below zero Celsius. This third law is especially important to scientists, but the first two laws are more important to us in the understanding of heat in our everyday lives.

Heat moves in three ways. They are called conduction, convection, and radiation. If you put a metal spoon in a glass of hot water, the spoon will get hot. When this happens, we say that the heat has moved by *conduction*. Heat flows by conduction when two things are touching.

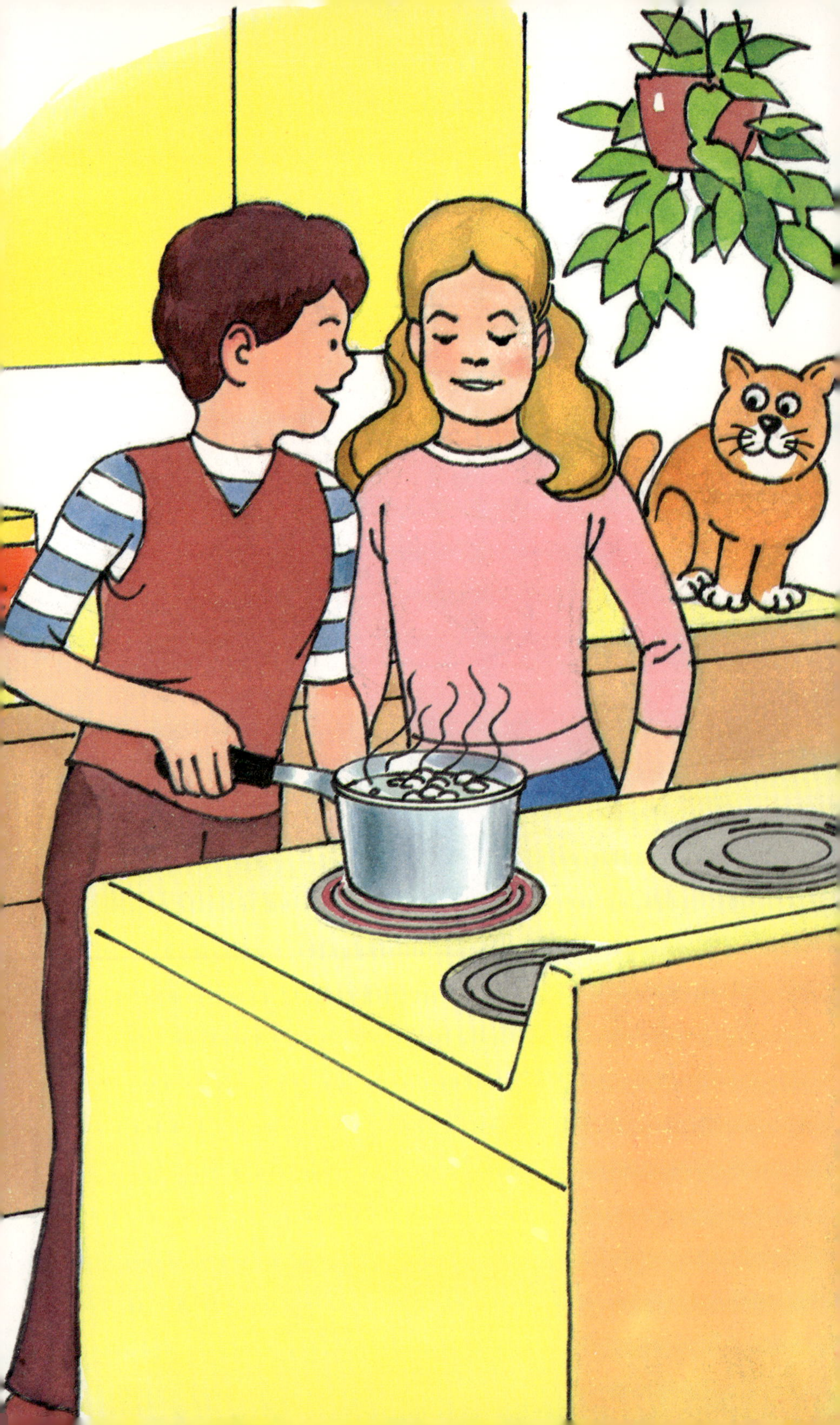

Some things conduct heat better than others. They are called good conductors. Metal is a good conductor, which is why many cooking pots are made of metal.

Other things do not conduct heat well. These are called bad conductors, or insulators. Wood is a bad conductor, which is why pot handles are sometimes made of wood. This lets you lift a very hot pot by its wooden handle without burning yourself.

When you heat a pot of water on a stove, the water at the bottom of the pot gets hot first. It expands and rises to the top. As the hot water rises, it pushes aside the colder water. The colder water sinks to replace the rising hot water. This keeps on happening until all the water is the same temperature.

The movement of rising heat and sinking cold is called *convection*. In nature, the heat of the sun warms masses of air near the Earth. When these heated air masses rise and masses of cooler air sink, we have convection currents called winds.

The third way heat moves is by *radiation*. The heat energy from the sun passes through space in the form of rays, or beams of radiation. When these rays reach us, we feel them as heat. When you feel the heat of the sun, you are taking in some of these heat rays. A rock standing in the sunlight will be much warmer than a rock in the shade. That is because the rock in sunlight has taken in more of the heat radiated by the sun.

The movement of heat into different things can change them. When you heat an ice cube, it changes into water. Then if you heat the water, it changes into a gas called steam or water vapor. But whether you have water in the form of a solid, a liquid, or a gas, it is still water. Only the form has changed.

Other things also change form when they are heated. Wax melts. So do butter and ice cream. If you apply enough heat you can even melt a solid metal bar. But cold will change all of them back into their original forms.

Heat can change some things in another way, so that they *cannot* be changed back into their original forms. When this happens it is because a chemical change has taken place. Once you burn a piece of wood, the ashes cannot be changed back into wood. When gasoline is burned in a car and converted into heat energy, the gasoline is gone for good.

When we eat, our bodies burn up the food, changing it into heat energy. This energy enables us to move, to grow, to keep warm, and to stay alive. Different foods have different amounts of energy to give. These amounts of energy are measured in units called *calories.* The more active we are, the more calories we burn up.

The number of calories you need depends on your size, how active you are, and how fast you are growing. You need enough calories to stay strong and healthy. But if you eat more calories than you can burn up, your body will store the extra calories as fat.

How important is heat? It runs our cars and planes and ships. It warms our schools, factories, stores, and homes. It cooks our food. It keeps us alive and healthy. So whether it's a hot fire or a hot bowl of soup…heat is very, very important to us all!